WELCOME TO THE WORLD OF

Wolverines

Diane Swanson

WALRUS
B O O K S

Edited by Elizabeth McLean
Proofread by Ben D'Andrea
Cover design by Steve Penner
Interior design by Margaret Ng
Typeset by Mark Macdonald & Jesse Marchand
Photo research by Mark Macdonald
Cover photograph by Daniel J. Cox / NaturalExpressions.com
Photo credits: Daniel J. Cox / NaturalExpressions.com

Printed and bound in China by WKT Company Ltd.

Library and Archives Canada Cataloguing in Publication

Swanson, Diane, 1944–
  Welcome to the world of wolverines / Diane Swanson.

  ISBN 1-55285-840-5
  ISBN 978-1-55285-840-0

  1. Wolverine—Juvenile literature. I. Title.
QL737.C25S93 2006   j599.76'6   C2006-900709-8

For more information on this series and other Whitecap Books titles, visit our website at www.whitecap.ca.

The publisher acknowledges the financial support of the Canada Council for the Arts, the British Columbia Arts Council, and the Government of Canada through the Book Publishing Industry Development Program (BPIDP). Whitecap Books also acknowledges the financial support of the Province of British Columbia through the Book Publishing Tax Credit.

Contents

World of Difference

THINK TOUGH. THINK WOLVERINE.
It's the most powerful member of the weasel family—and that even includes the brawny badger. In fact, for its size, the wolverine may be the strongest of the mammals. Although it's no bigger than a dog of medium height and weight, it can scare away a mountain lion and haul a deer up a tree.

A wolverine can resemble the cub of a black bear.

The super strength of the wolverine has given it several scary names, such as devil beast and evil spirit. What's more, some folks believe that it has a fiery temper. Others think that its hide has the power to make people hungry forever. But that's just folklore.

1

Even snow and ice don't soak a wolverine's thick coat.

After all, wolverines tend to avoid humans, so few people know the animal well.

Sometimes wolverines are mistaken for black bear cubs. With their little eyes, rounded ears, and boxy snouts, the wolverines look a lot like the cubs. They're also both very furry.

A wolverine's coat, like a black bear's coat, has two layers. The guard hair, or outer coat, can be 10 centimeters (4 inches) long. The woolly underfur, or inner coat, is a lot shorter. It grows extra thick in the winter, which helps to keep the animal warm.

Seen from behind, wolverines are almost never confused with black bear cubs. A wolverine's tail is much longer than a bear's stubby one. The thick, bushy tail of a wolverine can be one-fifth to one-quarter the length of its body, and it's covered with long hair.

WONDEROUS WOLVERINES

Wolverines are amazing. Here are a few of the reasons why:

- A wolverine is strong enough to drag an animal three times its weight down a mountain, across a river, and up a slope.

- In a single food-hiding spot, one wolverine stored as many as 100 birds.

- Wolverines sometimes use empty beaver lodges as their own hideaway homes.

- The outer hairs on a wolverine can shed frost, keeping its fur coat dry.

Where in the World

YOU AREN'T LIKELY TO SPOT WOLVERINES. They keep well away from cities and towns, preferring to spend their life in the wilderness. They exist in some of Earth's coldest climates—in the far north right around the globe. Wolverines live in places such as Alaska, Canada, Russia, Finland, Norway, and Sweden.

A lone wolverine travels the wilderness in search of food.

Each wolverine needs a huge area, or territory, mainly to find enough food to eat. Males need the most space as they go looking for both meals and mates. One female may have a territory that's 500 square kilometres (190 square miles).

Tired from walking, a wolverine slumps in an old tree.

But the territory of a male can be four times that size—2000 square kilometres (770 square miles).

Territories can overlap, especially if they are used by adult wolverines of the opposite sex or by adult wolverines and young ones. Two males or two females normally don't share part of a territory, but in some places they might.

A wolverine territory varies a lot. It can include soggy marshes, steep canyons, and thick mountain forests. It can also include open tundra—flat, treeless stretches of arctic land. Places that get buried under snow in fall and winter are often favorites.

How high or how low wolverines live also varies. And that can change from season to season. Many head to upper slopes in the summer. Some even go higher than levels where trees can grow. In winter, they might move lower down. The presence of both prey and predators affects where the wolverines go.

Wolverines don't spend much time together. Apart from mating and raising their families, they tend to wander their large world alone.

HIDING AWAY

Nap times for wolverines are spent in almost any shelter they can find. Within their own territories, they tend to rest for three or four hours among boulders and inside caves. Then they're up and away for the next three or four hours.

Wild storms or threats from enemies such as wolves can also make wolverines search for hideaways. Some have torn through the wood walls of hunters' sheds to get inside. There they settle down until danger has passed.

World in Motion

WOLVERINES WALK AND WALK AND WALK.
They break into gallops, too. Almost every
day, they haul their heavy bodies across long
distances. It's easy for wolverines to cover
more than 32 kilometres (20 miles) in a day.

Traveling hour after hour, wolverines
wander widely in search of meals. They
usually follow the same routes, heading back
to wherever they've discovered food before.
In winter, some might take trails that have
been cut by snowmobiles.

If wolves, bears, mountain lions, or
human hunters threaten wolverines, they
may try to race away. They can reach speeds

Climbing is no
problem for a
wolverine.

9

Sometimes a wolverine races so fast that its feet look blurry.

of 40 kilometres (25 miles) per hour. And they can keep running for up to 65 kilometres (40 miles) before stopping for a rest.

Moving over rough, mountainous land, wolverines plow through dense bush, swim rivers, and cross glaciers— masses of year-round snow and ice.

Even when winter temperatures plunge well below freezing, the animals keep on going.

Deep snow doesn't stop wolverines. Their large, flat feet act like snowshoes, and the hair on their soles keeps their feet warm. It also helps the animals grip slippery ground.

Sometimes wolverines use their strong legs to climb. With sharp, curved claws, they can clamber up tall trees. The view from high branches lets the wolverines see what's around them. Trees are also great places to escape from their enemies and, perhaps, to store food.

WOLVERINE WALKABOUT

It's hard to trail wolverines. That's why researchers outfit some of the animals with radio collars, then track the signals coming from those collars.

One male wolverine in Wyoming was studied for about two years. The animal wowed researchers. On one of his "short" walks, he made a 412-kilometre (256-mile) round trip between the states of Wyoming and Idaho. Less than a week later, he was off on another long trek, usually traveling through mountain forests at levels 2150 metres (7,000 feet) above sea level.

World of the Scavenger

LEFTOVERS MAKE MANY MEALS FOR WOLVERINES. Their dinners are often what mountain lions, bears, or wolves leave behind. After these hunters kill and eat large animals such as elk and moose, the wolverines feed on whatever remains. They aren't fussy eaters, even munching on hides and bones.

Wolverines are great scavengers—animals that feed on the dead—especially in winter. That's when other food can be hard to find. Sometimes, they follow hunters, trying to be nearby when prey is attacked. And by standing their hair

A wolverine feasts on the bones and hide that predators left behind.

Snarling and snapping, a wolverine displays its sharp teeth.

on end, raising their tails, and baring their teeth, the wolverines may be able to scare the hunters away. Then the wolverines take over the prey before the meat is all gone.

Animals that have died from diseases or accidents also make meals for wolverines. Along sea coasts, they feast on the bodies of whales, walruses, and seals that float up on shores. The wolverines don't get sick from eating flesh that's rotting.

Wolverines have an amazing sense of smell. They can easily sniff out dead animals. In fact, they can smell bodies that are buried deep beneath the snow.

Like all meat-eaters, wolverines seldom know when they'll dine again. Several days may pass between meals, so the wolverines must live on the fat stored in their bodies. That's why they stuff themselves as much as possible whenever they can. Besides keeping them alive, the scavenging ways of wolverines help clean up their world.

AWESOME BITE

Gnaw thick hooves. Grind bones to powder. Crunch chunks of solidly frozen flesh. None of these jobs challenges a wolverine. After all, it has powerful neck muscles, a huge head, and large jaws that are super strong.

As well, 38 big teeth equip the wolverine for heavy-duty chewing. It grows upper molars (grinding teeth) that angle inward, so the wolverine can crush almost anything. Not surprisingly, it's famous for its awesome bite. CHOMP!

World of the Hunter

WOLVERINES CHASE THEIR OWN CHOW, TOO—although they make better scavengers than they do hunters.

During warm months, wolverines snack on what they can find. That can include berries, roots, and eggs. And they hunt critters that are smaller than themselves, attacking frogs, mice, chipmunks, ground squirrels, geese, hares, foxes, beavers—even porcupines. However, wolverines have died from swallowing the quills of porcupines.

With their great sense of smell, wolverines have no trouble sniffing out prey. Using their sturdy front legs and long claws, they

Gotcha! With its wide paws, a wolverine nabs a mouse in early spring.

17

A wolverine searches for a place to hide its prey.

dig through soil, turn over rocks, or rip open logs. They pounce on some animals and gallop after others. One blow from the powerful paws of wolverines is often enough to kill their prey.

In winter, a wolverine's wide furry paws carry it easily across the snow. That helps it hunt larger animals such as deer that can't move well through deep drifts. Occasionally, these larger animals become completely stuck. When a wolverine strikes, it normally bites the prey on the back of the neck.

Sometimes, a hunting wolverine might rest along a tree branch, then drop down on an unsuspecting mountain sheep. Other times, the hunter stages an ambush, leaping from behind a boulder or bush. Whatever its method, the wolverine kills mostly for food.

STOCKING UP

Wolverines often hide food to eat later. They usually bury it, digging holes in soft ground. Their hiding places, called caches (KASH-ez), may also be under snow, between rocks, or in trees. They often store food close to dens so it's handy for young wolverines.

Marking caches as their own is important to wolverines. But that doesn't stop them from looting the caches of foxes, bears, or people. Like other animals, wolverines sometimes steal food when they're hungry.

World of Words

NO WONDER WOLVERINES ARE CALLED SKUNK BEARS. They're stinky—but for good reason. Wolverines leave smells around as messages, although they don't fire them out the way skunks do.

A wolverine uses the strong smells from its own urine and dung, and the ooze from its glands to create signals. Glands on its face, belly, and rear end produce a stinky substance. It also has glands on the bottoms of its hind feet.

Marking rocks, trees, and logs, the wolverine rubs or deposits smells where it wants to leave a signal. The wolverine might

Two kits growl their messages to each other.

Smelly footprints in the snow announce that a wolverine has gone by.

also put an odor on top of scents left by another animal, such as a coyote. But the glands in the wolverine's back feet likely leave odors wherever it walks, making a l-o-n-g message that says where it's been.

Messages might be placed near food to claim it. "Mine. All mine," they seem to announce. Some smells mean, "Back off. Leave me alone."

Other odors are used to mark territories. When a wolverine is roaming a distant part of its territory, the smells it leaves behind signal its claim.

Scent signals are handy, especially in places such as forests where it can be hard to hear or see far. The smells that wolverines leave tend to last well. And they have the noses needed to sniff out what others are saying to them.

Wolverines also talk a bit through sounds, such as grunts, usually to their kits, and the kits often growl in play. Still, as they spend a lot of time wandering large areas alone, wolverines spread most of their news and claims through odors.

SIGNING THE WOLVERINE WAY

Wolverines studied in Montana left about eight signs for each kilometre (more than half a mile) they walked. Sometimes they made signs by scraping the soil. Now and then they bit roots or branches. Occasionally, they marked the ground with stinky things, such as ooze or dung.

No one is sure exactly what these messages meant. But the most common signs were smells left near or on tree trunks. Once in a while, the wolverines climbed the trees before "signing" them.

New World

MOST WOLVERINE KITS HAVE SPRING BIRTHDAYS.
They're usually born in late March, along
with one or two sisters or brothers each.

The birth den is a simple one. It might be
a shallow pit, cave, or hollow tree. It might
also be a tunnel that a mother has dug in the
snow. Small cubbyholes along a snow tunnel
can be used to store food for the wolverines.

Weighing no more than a medium-sized
apple, a kit is born helpless. Its eyes are
tightly closed and no teeth are showing.
However, the kit arrives in a thick coat of
woolly white fur.

For 8 to 10 weeks, wolverine kits feed

From their rocky
den, kits take a
peek at their new
world.

It's a fun time when
wolverine kits play
together.

hungrily on their mother's milk. During
that time, she may move them from
den to den. She carries the kits gently
by the loose skin on the backs of their
necks. Melting snow or threats from
nearby enemies can be reasons for
changing house.

When wolverine kits are big enough

to walk with their mother, they follow her on trips to find food. At first, they stick close. But when they're about six months old, they begin scouting the woods by themselves. Although mother wolverines care for the young kits, a few scientists think that adult males may find and guide older ones.

Wolverine kits grow quickly, reaching their full size before their first birthday. Still, some of them stay with their families until they're two. Then they head off to find their own territories.

Life in the big world is seldom easy for wolverines, but if they're lucky, they might live 10 years.

ROMPING WOLVERINES

There's no doubt about it. Wolverine kits like rolling around in the snow. If there's no snow, no problem. The kits also enjoy rolling on the ground.

When they play together, two wolverine kits often tease each other. They pretend to wrestle, then bat their heads, and tug their ears. When one climbs a short tree, it might suddenly hurl itself down and nibble the hair of another kit. Then the two wolverines might grab a stick and play tug of war—all in fun.

Index